SID WADDELL

TAAK

OF THE

TOON

HOW TO SPEAK
GEORDIE

HarperCollins Publishers
The News Building
1 London Bridge Street
London
SE1 9GF

www.collinslanguage.com

First Edition 2008

ISBN 978-0-00-724782-0

A catalogue record for this
book is available from the
British Library.

Designed by Wolfgang Homola

Typeset by Thomas Callan

Editorial Staff
Cormac McKeown
Ian Brookes
Lucy Cooper
Robert Groves

Introduction

Everybody thinks their own bit of Britain is the best. I have Cockney pals who swear their hospitality and wit are the tops. A mate of mine from Nottingham swore the best ale and the prettiest lasses could be found within a couple of miles of the Lace Market. 'Rubbish!' would be the verdict of West Country pals who would attest that their scrumpy, songs, and cheeses are unbeatable.

So what would a proud Geordie like myself crack up about the place, the people and the lifestyle? Well, we do welcome strangers like long-lost friends. We do have ales like the Broon that put a buzz on your visit and nosh, like stotties, to beef you up. Our lasses are as bonny and lippy as any and the lads are boisterous, aggressive-sounding, but often as soft as thistle-down. But our main talent as a tribe is verbal: Geordies, I reckon, word-for-word could out-patter anybody.

And this brings me to my main reason for writing **TAAK OF THE TOON**. At moments of high emotion and/or excitement I lapse into Geordie, despite living in Yorkshire for the past 38 years. That, I would suggest, is testimony to the sheer richness of our language. Some of our words date back to invaders who hit Bamburgh and North Shields 1300 years ago. Down the centuries we have melded in Dutch, Scottish and Romany words to articulate the vivid Geordie life-experience.

So tek a deep breath, rax yer tonsils, clear yer clack... and dive in, marras.

THE ENTIRE GEORDIE NATION

There was a very loud Newcastle rock band in the 1960s called 'The Entire Sioux Nation'; nobody slept in the entire Toon when the lads were on the go. Dogs howled, workers wakened from bonny dreams cursed and burglars ran home with empty pokes.

The best way to regard the Geordie Nation is to parallel it with the American Indians: massive hunting and marauding tribes like the Sioux, the Apache and the Comanche. Within each of those proud fierce groups there were regional sub-divisions who fought to the death over buffalo killing rights, theft of horses and the odd bit of squaw-pinching. However, though we Geordies talk with pals as though a fight is about to erupt, divvent youse worry. Our patter is merely torrential enthusiasm and we don't fight foreigners often.

The Geordie Nation's heartland is Newcastle, alias The Toon, with its long trading, seafaring and ship building traditions. From Scotswood to Wallsend we have the ancestral home of the Toony Geordies. They are descendants of blue-bonneted keel men; flash guys quick to take the piss out of pit village lads. See a rag and bone man clopping and calling doon Westgate Road and you see a patter merchant, a verbal chancer. Modern Newcastle is the Mecca for Hens and Stags from all over

Britain and the chat on the Quayside is all the richer for it. It is also possible to theorise that the number nine shirt worn by the centre forward of Newcastle United is a mythical totem-like symbol. Players like Hughie Gallacher, Jackie Milburn, Malcolm McDonald and Alan Shearer are to the Geordie tribe what Yellow Hand, Crazy Horse, Cochise, and Geronimo were to the American Indians – the peak of our manhood, role models and heroes.

Travel a few miles north of the Tyne and you find the Pitmatic Geordies: the branch of the tribe who once worked the coal mines round Ashington, Bedlington and Blyth. This lot talk as though they had a mouthful of iron filings and broken glass. I am a proud paid-up member of this branch, being bred in Ashington where my father worked down the pit for 48 years. Though the flash guys live in the Toon, the racy chat of the hard-grafting miners is probably the most vivid seam of Geordie language.

To the north and west of this branch, in Morpeth and Alnwick, we find the Romany influence in the Gadgie Geordies. Their main business was horse trading and they had many connections across the Pennines with Appleby and Carlisle. Some of their wild blood flows in my veins since I was born in Alnwick and my pipe-smoking granny spoke a lot of hawker/gipsy patter. **'Deek the gadgie with the radge jugal and the cushty mort.'** Translation: 'Look at the man with the mad dog and the comely maiden.'

Even further west we have the Coonty Geordies, the wealthy self-employed farmers, folk who have tended to look down on the poorer, more collective-minded branches of the tribe who dug the coal, built the ships, caught the fish, and manned the boats. These people think 'sex' is what the coal is delivered in.

South of the Tyne and at its mouth we have the Sand Dancer Geordies. Some people regard them as Mackems, but most South Shields folk I know are proud to be called Geordies.

To the south of Geordieland, in what was once the old county of Durham, lies the land of the Mackems. They are so-called because they say 'mack' instead of 'make' and 'tack' instead of 'take'. They are enemies of the Geordies, particularly on the football field. But a lot of them in Gateshead and the East Durham pit villages talk like us. So the inter-tribal violence is mostly satirical or symbolic.

The folk of Teesside are known as Smoggies, because of the rotten smelly fug that hangs like a manky shroud over their polluted river.

To the north of the Geordies live the Jocks, whose words you will read here because we swiped a lot of them. They are not really wor enemies, because to many Scots 'a Geordie is just a Jock with his heid kicked in'.

I mention these other tribes because we Geordies have often defined ourselves as enemies of the lesser breeds south and north of the Rio Grande – the Mighty Tyne. But really, as this book will show once you get to know us, we are deed canny… as lang as we get wor own way!

aad *adjective* old

aakward *adjective* awkward

aal *adjective* all

aalreet *adverb, adjective* all right
Compare **reet**

I can hear yee aalreet but my lugs are not reet aalreet. Aalreet?

TRANSLATION: I am at odds with you, myself and the entire world. OK?

afore *adverb, preposition, conjugation*
before

Afore oppenin yer gob, use yer noddle.

TRANSLATION: Engage brain before speaking.

agyen *adverb* again

ahad *noun* **1** a hold | *adjective, adverb* **2** on fire [From Geordie pronunciation of *hold*]

Tyek ahad of me hand and ah'll lead yer to the land of your dreams.

TRANSLATION: Come with me to the deeper parts of Jesmond Dene.

Ah've hoyed matches and paraffin on this bliddy fire but it winnit tyek ahad.

TRANSLATION: We have to put on woollies because I cannot get the fire to light.

aheyt *adverb, adjective* in the air
[Probably from Geordie pronunciation of *height*]

In pitch and toss yee hoy two coins up aheyt and cross yer fingers.

TRANSLATION: Gambling is not a reliable form of occupation.

ahint *preposition, adverb* behind
[From Old English *aethindan*]

amang *preposition* among

Aladdin must have been reet dim

to faal amang them gadgies.

TRANSLATION: Aah the innocence
of youth.

argie *verb* to argue

Yee would argie yer way through
the Hobs of Hell.

TRANSLATION: Your disputative
nature will bring you to a very sad
end.

arly *adjective* early

arn *verb* to earn

atween *preposition* between

Ah feel ah'm atween a rock and a
hard place.

TRANSLATION: The wife and the
mother-in-law are in cahoots against
me.

aye¹ *sentence substitute* yes [Old English *a* always]. *Compare* **aye²**

aye² *adverb* always; ever [Old Norse *ei* ever]

> **Yer aye deein that!**
> TRANSLATION: Why not try to introduce some variety into proceedings?

ayont *preposition* beyond

> **Hey bonny lad, that's weel ayont a joke.**
> TRANSLATION: Your attempt to flatter me with humour is an insult.

WELCOME STRANGER

Despite the violent sounding gutturals, glottal stops and in-yer-face delivery of us Geordies, we are a hospitable tribe, ever ready to welcome lads and lasses who come smoking the pipe of peace. Travellers will be greeted with the traditional warming cry: **'Gittheroondin kidda!'**[1]

So, before pointing your painted pony at our heartlands, here are a few key words and expressions to ease your entry into Geordie society.

I will dramatise your first few likely encounters with the locals: first, you alight for your weekend at Newcastle Central

Station and wish to leave your luggage so you can begin *staggering* or *henning* right off. I suggest you approach the person on the pasty stall thus: '**Heypet cannahoyme-bagahinttheor?**'[2]

Almost certainly the answer will be: '**Naebotheratallcaacanny.**'[3] If it's Saturday you will be surrounded by hundreds of human zebras – Toon fans proudly strutting in their black and white tops. Approach them boldly with a cheesy grin and say: '**Hoozit gannagan athgyemthiday bonnyladz?**'[4]

Once they see you are not a Mackem spy they will lead you willingly to their favourite watering holes with this encouraging cry: '**Howay alang wiusfor-rabevvy.**'[5]

Once in the Strawberry or the Bacchus,

both decked out with photos of United legends, they will ask, 'Reet marra deeyeewant broon or ex?', refining the idea possibly thus, 'Offtheneck – orbyglass, streyt or kinky?'[6]

I would advise that after a few pints you seek food. Approach the barmaid and say, 'Ahmscrannyhevyeeanystotties?'[7] She might reply like this, 'Areyeesum radgie gadgie? nee mebbesabootit…wees hoachin withem.'[8]

When the food appears, thank her profusely and tip her. 'Ta petgit yersella pint when yeetek yer blaa.'[9]

Having satisfied the inner man or woman you may now proceed bravely and merrily among the locals.

Glossary

1 'Buy the beers and you've got mates for life.'

2 'Pardon me, friendly-looking person, but may I deposit my luggage on your premises?'

3 'My pleasure, have a nice day'.

4 'Are you confident of a Newcastle victory in today's soccer contest?'

5 'Join us for a libation or several.'

6 'Righto, pal, are you drinking Brown Ale or Exhibition? If you need a glass do you want a sleeve or a handle?'

7 'I am hungry. Have you any local sandwiches?'

8 'What a daft question! If we had any more sarnies in here there'd be no room for punters.'

9 'Pray take a sherbet on me during your break.'

baary *adjective* lovely [From Romany. Compare Scots *barry*]

> **We had a baary time at Whitley Bay even though we lost aal wor lowey at the shows.**
> TRANSLATION: Our visit to the coast was fun even though we got skint at the funfair.

babby *noun* a baby, infant, or toddler

> **You're sticking that top lip oot like a little babby.**
> TRANSLATION: Grow up!

baccy chow *noun* chewing tobacco [From *baccy* tobacco + *chow* to chew]

> **Yee are not worth a baccy chow.**
> TRANSLATION: You do not rank in my spectrum of esteemed persons.

badly *adjective* in poor health; sick; ill

> **If ye weren't badly ah'd clock yer one.**
> TRANSLATION: Your illness is an excuse for getting away with murder.

baggie *noun* a stickleback or other small fish

> **You're nowt but a tatty baggie in yer own little pond.**
> TRANSLATION: There is a great big world out there, sonny.

bagie *noun* a turnip [From Swedish *(rota)bagge*]

bairn *noun* a child [From Old English *bearn*]

bait *noun* food, esp a packed lunch [From Old Norse *beita* hunt]

bargie *verb* **1** to claim | *interjection* **2 bargies me!** bagsy!

> **Bargies me that doggie in the window.**
> TRANSLATION: I wish that scruffy

mongrel could be our family pet.

barry *verb* to bury

> **Ah want to barry the hatchet – in his bliddy heed.**
>
> TRANSLATION: The quality of mercy is extremely strained.

bat *noun* **1** a blow | *verb* **2** to hit (someone or something) [From French *battre*]

batchy *adjective* extremely angry; furious [probably related to *batty*]

> **Me mother went batchy when I got me new troosers hacky playing muggies.**
>
> TRANSLATION: Mama was not best pleased at the state of my pants after playing marbles.

belly-topper *noun* a young woman wearing an outfit that exposes her midriff

> **Deek thon belly-topper; yee can see aal hor knickors and half her knockors!**
> TRANSLATION: Look at that young lady! Her attire leaves little to the imagination.

beor *noun* beer

bide *verb* to wait

big end *noun* the concert room in a pub or club. *Compare* **tit-and-fiddle end**

> **The big end is stowed off, so we'll hev to slum it in the bar.**
> TRANSLATION: Do we really need to hear that comedian again?

bingo dobber *noun* a round felt pen used to mark bingo cards [Perhaps from Geordie pronunciation of *dab* or *daub*]

> **Wor Markie is about as sharp as a bingo dobber.**
> TRANSLATION: Brother Mark is no Einstein.

biv *preposition, adverb* by. *Compare* **divvent**

> **Ah've come to this club biv mesell cos ah nivvor score when ah'm wi the lads.**
> TRANSLATION: Lone wolves strike luckiest.

blaa *verb* **1** to blow | *noun* **2** breath; a rest [Northern pronunciation of *blow*]

The wind is blaain see hard we'd better tek a blaa behind the dyke.
TRANSLATION: Let us shelter from the elements.

blackclock *noun* a cockroach [From *black* + *clock* (an obsolete or dialect word for any beetle)]

bleb *noun* a swelling on human skin that is smaller than a blob; a blister [Possibly a shortening of *blob* a bubble or blister]

I hoyed the coal in till me hands were aal blebby.
TRANSLATION: Hard work has its problems.

blether *verb* **1** to waffle; talk nonsense | *noun* **2** nonsense [From Old Norse *blathr* nonsense]

blethered *adjective* wearied;
exhausted

bletherskite *noun* a compulsive
talker [From *blether* to talk nonsense +
skite a detestable person]

> **That bletherskite is mekkin me
> lugs hort.**
> TRANSLATION: Please connect brain
> before engaging gob.

blogged *adjective* blocked

> **Wor drains is blogged and there's
> a reet stink.**
> TRANSLATION: Avoid our place of
> residence in the immediate future.

bogey *noun* **1** a small non-
motorized vehicle made by small
children; a go-cart **2** a large motor
vehicle used to transport industrial

materials [Perhaps related to *buggy*, originally a two-wheeled horse-drawn vehicle]

> **Wor kid's bogey is made of orange boxes and pram wheels.**
> TRANSLATION: My brother's go-cart is no Beamer.

boily *noun* **1** soup **2** a hot drink made with milk and pieces of bread, given especially to infants and sick people [From French *bouillon*]

bone *verb* to ask (someone) a question [Perhaps related to *boon* a request or favour asked]

> **Ah'm ganna bone him aboot that bet. Mebbees he nivvor put it on...**
> TRANSLATION: Perhaps he trousered

our money knowing the horse had no chance.

bonny *adjective* **1** beautiful or handsome **2** excellent; first rate **3** drunk [French *bon* good]

> **Yee were bonny last neet, yer legs were plaited.**
> TRANSLATION: The alcohol you drank did nothing to help your dancing style.

bool *noun* **1** a bowl **2 on the bool** on a drinking session | *verb* **3** to have sex

> **He had a bool of porridge then went oot on the bool.**
> TRANSLATION: He filled up on oats and went out to sow them.

bord *noun* **1** a bird **2** a young woman

borst *verb* burst

> **Had yer rotten tongue or ah'll borst yer gob.**
> TRANSLATION: Silence is advisable unless you'd like a visit to intensive care.

bouldy-hole *noun* a glory hole; coal hole

bowdy-kite *noun* a pot belly
[Perhaps from *bowl* and *kite* meaning 'belly']

> **Are yee expectin', Mavis, or is that bowdy-kite doon to the Broon?**
> TRANSLATION: Is your protuberance down to procreation or recreation?

bowk *verb* **1** to belch **2** to vomit [From Middle English *bolken*]

bray *verb* to thrash; beat up [From Old French *breier* break, pound]

breed *noun* bread

broon *or* **Broon** *noun* Newcastle Brown Ale

bubble *verb* to cry

bubbly-jock *noun* a turkey [Perhaps rhyming slang for 'turkey cock']

bullet *noun* a type of small sweet [Purportedly because they resemble the bullets that killed Nelson]

bummlor *noun* a bumblebee

> He dances as though he had a bummlor doon his keks.

TRANSLATION: Give that man 100% for effort.

byek *verb* to bake

byeuts *plural noun* boots

Wor Chick gans ti the dance in his pit byeuts, sez it stops the lasses daddin' his toes.

TRANSLATION: My friend is more practical than stylish.

WOR HISTORY AND WOR HEROES

I suppose the first Geordie was the Venerable Bede who sat in his monastery at Jarrow about 1200 years ago and described the pillaging Vikings in much the same way as Toon football supporters describe the Mackem hordes: daft lads who go berserk after a couple of lager shandies. There is, in his works and the writings of his isolated pals on Lindisfarne, a sense of tribe that has come down through the ages, a sense of 'ganging up' against the rest of a hostile world. I like to think of Bedey and a few of his muckers drying off their quills, sloughing off their hair shirts and swanning along to a pleasant Saturday night hop in Bamburgh. Drop of mead, quick Gay Gordons with the local talent, then back in time for a cold shower and a mumbled matins…

Moving to the colourful hectic age that Shakespeare immortalized, we have the doughty figure of Harry Hotspur, a cross between Lord Lucan and Arthur Scargill, part wild-child, part local hero. He spent his time fighting for whatever king was in power in London or sitting in Warkworth Castle planning to join the Jocks and invade London. Harry also had a terrible problem with pronouncing his Rs. So his granny made up this verbal mantra – one that many of us still use as an exercise today. 'Roond the rugged rock the ragged rascal ran.' It is best attempted by pushing out the cheeks like a hungry gorilla and trying to get imaginary claggum (chewing gum) off the base of the tongue.

The identity of Geordies became crystallized as sea-borne trade, particularly in coal, developed on the Tyne. Nowadays the 'bonny lads' who strut their stuff along the Quayside are rich footballers, legal eagles or IT wizards – all fat knots and designer stubble – but around 1750 the cocks of the walk were keelmen. These were an elite band of experts who rowed boats full of coal to and from merchant sailing ships in the Tyne. They had their own guild and their badge of honour was a blue bonnet, set off with a red neckerchief and silver shoe buckles. They earned top dollar, were known to enjoy a swallow or three, and occasionally broke the hearts of the ladies.

Nobody knows why the legendary 'Bonny' Bobby Shaftoe – trained on keels but later a seafarer – went off over the briny, but I reckon it was to do with sex or drink or debt – or all the above. Our bright-eyed verbalized romanticism has always been deeply shadowed by excess.

In 2005 Northumberland County Council ran a 'Most Famous Northumbrians' website competition and polled 30,000 people. This was the result:

George Stephenson. He was the man who put a Rocket up the pants of the transport system by inventing a viable track-based steam locomotive. His mother kept shouting, **'Stop clocking that bliddy kettle, Georgie, ye knaa it'll nivvor bile.'** Translation: 'Get out of the house and do some useful work, you waster.'

Grace Darling. Did the single sculls out of a harbour in a fierce storm and rescued people from a foundering ship.

Lord Armstrong. Famous arms and munitions maker with a factory along the old Scotswood road. Turned 'Cragside' at Rothbury into a turreted mansion sporting the latest electric and hydraulic gadgets. Typical saying: **'What do yee lot want with a union? Stand on yer own pasties!'** Translation: 'I'm alright, Jacks.'

Jane, Duchess of Northumberland. Smart lassie who persuaded the government to give her £14 million to create a massive natural jewel of a garden in the backyard of Alnwick Castle.

Jackie Milburn. The greatest centre forward Newcastle ever had. Scored six goals in a trial match having come from

Ashington on the bus with his boots in a carrier bag.

Jack Charlton. Another Ashingtonian who was in England's World Cup-winning team of 1966 and now hunts, shoots and fishes like a squire of old.

Sid Waddell. Bloke who cracks daft jokes while posing as a darts commentator.

Capability Brown. Designer of fancy gardens for posh folk. Could have done the Alnwick Castle job for thirty bob and free beer!

Thomas Bewick. South Tyne etching genius who drew beautiful British bords (feathered variety).

Sir Bobby Charlton. Soccer legend.

A mixed bag, you will agree. I was dead chuffed to be included. Due to the poll being only for Northumbrians, famous

Toonies were left out. I would add: Jimmy Nail – 'a right scunner' (moody person); Ant and Dec; Bryan Ferry; Mark Knopfler; Gazza – daft as a brush; Sting – 'more edge than a broken piss pot' (deluded by self-importance); Eric Burdon; and Cheryl Tweedy.

For my money the most vivid image of the typical Geordie was Bobby Thompson, alias the Little Waster, comedian extraordinaire. Bobby was a radio star in the 1940s and 50s on a show called *What Cheor* (Cheer) *Geordie*. He played a lazy, sneaky, above all boozy ched (low-life) who depended on his long-suffering wife Phyllis, but never gave her the lickings of a dog (faint praise).

My favourite Bobby story concerns a night when he came out of retirement for one night only to do a special gig up West Durham. As the warm-up acts did their thing, Bobby was a bag of nerves and wolfed down Bloody Marys and beetroot sandwiches. He was greeted wildly on stage, only to vomit red gunk all over the microphone. Quick as a flash the Concert Secretary, all Brylcreem and Old Spice, was on the microphone. 'What a trooper is the Little Waster – his stomach ulcer borsts on stage but he is ettled (determined) that the show must go on.' Cue more wild applause and the performance of Bobby's life.

The Jocks would call Bobby a *chancer*, and we would call him a *mazer* (phenomenon).

caa *verb* **1** push, pull, or otherwise move (something) **2 caa canny** to proceed with caution; take care **3 gan on the caa canny** to work to rule [From *call* (in the Scots sense, meaning 'to drive')]

Caa canny with that pick or you'll caa the roof down.

TRANSLATION: Please respect the coal strata above us; I'd prefer that it stayed there.

caald *adjective* cold

cacky *noun* excrement [From Latin *cacare*, perhaps via Dutch *kakken*, to defecate]

canna *verb* cannot

canny *adjective* nice; agreeable [From *can* (in the sense 'to know how'), from Old English *cunnan*]

Ah've got a canny good number and the foreman's canny as weel.

TRANSLATION: I'm a lazy sod and my supervisor could not give a toss either.

caunch *noun* **1** a ridge or bank in a pit **2** a woman's buttocks [From the English dialect word *canch*, a step-like stone in a coal pit]

cavil *noun* a miner's designated work area; rotated regularly to ensure an even share of working conditions among the miners [Related to Dutch *kavel* lot; the work areas were assigned by lot]

champion *adjective, sentence substitute* great!; excellent

> **I hev three broken ribs and a hernia but ah feel champion.**
> TRANSLATION: You should see the other fellow.

chare *noun* a narrow alleyway [From Old English *cerran* to turn]

"She's got chollers like Scooby Doo!" ▶

charva *noun* **1** a man **2** sex [From Romany *chavo*]

> **I reckon that bonny charva is only after a quick charva.**
> **TRANSLATION:** He looks the sort of laddo who will have his way then not even buy you a fish supper.

ched *noun* a wastrel

chimla *noun* a chimney

chollers *plural noun* jowls [From Old English *ceolor* throat]

> **She's got lovely eyes but chollers like Scooby Doo.**
> **TRANSLATION:** I bet kissing her is like snogging a goldfish.

chowk *verb* to choke

> **Me mother made us gargle wi**

mustard, but all it did was mek us chowk.

TRANSLATION: Mater's knowledge of medicine is extremely basic.

clack *noun* the uvula [From Middle English *clack-en*]

claes *plural noun* clothes [From Scots]

He thinks we divvent notice but he gets aal his claes from the Oxfam shop.

TRANSLATION: He is rarely seen at Top Man or Gap.

clag¹ *verb* to stick to (something) [perhaps from Old Norse]

clag² *verb* to hit (somebody) [Perhaps referring to the sound of a blow, as with certain senses of *clack*]

claggy *adjective* sticky [See *clag*[1]]

> **If this taffy was a bit more claggy me teeth would stick together.**
> TRANSLATION: I asked for a treat not a gumshield.

clarts *plural noun* (lumps of) mud [From Middle English *biclarten* to soil]

> **That bairn could find clarts in the Sahara Desert.**
> TRANSLATION: The child is a mud-magnet.

clash *noun, verb* gossip [A dialect usage of *clash* in the sense of 'loud noise']

> **Wor mother would stop for a clash even if her arse was on fire.**
> TRANSLATION: Mother cannot resist verbal social intercourse.

cleg *noun* a gadfly or horse-fly [From Old Norse *kleggi*]

> **You are as much fun as a cleg up a nostril.**
> TRANSLATION: I find you a social irritant.

clemmy *or* **clemmie** *noun* a stone

> **Alreet we'll hev a street barney, but just fists, nee clemmies.**
> TRANSLATION: Let battle commence but we'll adhere to Queensbury Rules.

cloot, clooty *or* **clout** *noun* a cloth [From Old English *clūt* a piece of metal or cloth]

cogley *adjective* **1** wobbly, shaky, or otherwise unsteady **2** crooked or slanted [Perhaps related to Welsh *gogi* to shake]

I went to the boozer like a
guardsman but ah cam hyem aal
cogley.

TRANSLATION: Aah, the transitions
produced by the hop and the grain.

coo *noun* a cow

cordy *noun* a penis [From Romany]

Caal that a cordy? I've seen better
specimens craal oot of cabbages.

TRANSLATION: I bet you have a nice
personality.

cowp *verb* 1 to tip 2 **cowp yer
boily** to vomit 3 **cowp yer
creels** to perform a forward roll
[From Old French *colper* to strike]

If ah cowp me creels, will yee dee
a stannin lowp?

TRANSLATION: If I do a forward roll
will you do a standing long jump?

crack¹ *noun* talk; chat

crack² *verb* to brag, boast, or otherwise aggrandize oneself

> **To hear her crack on the Duke of Northumberland comes roond for tea ivvery day.**
>
> TRANSLATION: Some folk will say owt for effect.

cracket *noun* a stool [a variant of *cricket*, a stool]

cree *noun* a shed [related to Old Norse *kra* a fold, and Irish *cro*]

> **There's nee pigeons nor hens in wor workingmen's club but we still call it the cree.**
>
> TRANSLATION: Our drinking gaffe is very cosy and basic when it comes to appurtenances.

croggie *noun* a ride or lift on a bicycle, especially when sitting on the crossbars

> **Give us a kiss and I'll give yee a croggie.**
> TRANSLATION: Jove's winged chariot awaits you, pet.

cuddy *noun* a donkey or pony [From *Cuddy*, a nickname for *Cuthbert*.]

cundy *noun* a drain [From French *conduit*]

custy *adjective* tasty [From Romany *kushti* fine]

cut *noun* a narrow passageway or alley, especially one between houses

> **Cut doon the first cut, miss the second, then cut right at the third.**

TRANSLATION: You have asked a right clever bugger for directions.

cyeuk *verb* **1** to cook | *noun* **2** a cook

WAALKING AND WORKING

There are traditonally two types of Geordie male: the one who is work-shy and the one who is a hard grafter.

The former have their ethos symbolized thus: '**Work? He canna *WAALK* nivvor mind work.**' Translation: 'The work ethic has left him by and is beyond his imaginative ken.'

Thank God the other ethos has inspired generations to build ships and bridges, dig coal, puddle steel, work farms and nurture and feed the living process.

Four hundred years ago there was not a lot of regular employment to be had in

Geordieland, so families like the Armstrongs, Robsons, Scotts, and Charltons of the Cheviot area devised an industry of their own. It was called reiving (taking by force). Come the Hunter's Moon in mid-October, the lady of the manor would turn a drinking tankard upside down on the table to indicate that meat and drink had run out. So, the menfolk had to put on armour and go and steal other folk's sheep and cattle. Usually this meant a trip to Jockland, but at a pinch, a quick foray against the Cumbrians or the worky-ticket (argumentative) family next door would suffice.

To this day a beer glass turned upside down in a Geordie bar still means, **'Ah'm fighting fit and will bray anybody in here willing to take me on.'** Translation: 'Come over here if you think you're hard enough.'

Farming is the staple industry of the north and west of our area and has given the language one of its most vivid verbal images. **'Caa hacky through the watter.'** Literally translated this means, 'Pull, push or otherwise move the dirty cow across the stream.' Also I, and many Geordie kids, used to spend much of the school holidays **'tetty howking'**, i.e. 'digging potatoes' for pocket money.

The Tyne was once one of the great shipbuilding rivers of the world. A proud tradition grew up of giant ships that rose from the stocks and dwarfed the houses of Wallsend. The Boilermaker's Society was second only to the National Union of Miners as the greatest trade union in the world. And brotherhood between nations was fostered in the noise and welding flame of the great Tyneside yards. Once a Japanese delegation arrived at Swan Hunters and after a few hours thanked the bosses for teaching the local lads Japanese in their honour.

'I divvent knaa what you mean,' said a mystified Swan executive.

'Worker over there clearly shouted to mate, *"HEYLAD HOYTHAT HAMMER OWERHEER",* explained the Japanese bloke. 'Perfectly understandable in Yokohama as "transfer the hammer to me aerially".'

But the industry that has contributed most to the Geordie lingo is coal-mining. Indeed, there are now books devoted to the study of pit jargon, known as 'Pitmatic'. The phrase 'on the trot', meaning consecutive, comes from the rope in a mine to which full tubs of coal were attached. Similarly 'caunch', meaning 'mound of earth' in the pit, now means male or female rump, e.g. 'We cud git to the bar if Elsie would shift her caunch oot the way.' Again, 'upcast' which referred to a pit's ventilation system, is used to describe the cause of a quarrel, e.g. 'If yee upcast that to me I'll borst yer gob.'

In this day and age the heavy industry is gone, but the heavy patter is still in evidence. A hen party might well expect this from a trendy young Byker blade as he mixes their Flaming Ferrari cocktails. 'I hev nivvor clapped eyes on such custy talent and yee divvent haff taak nice.' Meaning: 'I'll be out of here and full of the bull at midnight, so apply moderation to your merriment.'

dad *verb* **1** to hit (something)
against (something else) **2** a blow

> **If yee fetch yor dad oot to hit me,
> ah'll get my dad to give your dad
> a dad on the lug.**
>
> TRANSLATION: Fight your own
> battles lest half the street should join
> the ruckus.

daffy *verb* to make oneself look neater; to dress smart

> **She's only gannin' to the bingo, but she's daffied up big time.**
> TRANSLATION: You've got to get wear out of your best clothes.

daftie *noun* a person who is daft; a fool

> **There's many a daftie made a bob or two.**
> TRANSLATION: Fortune favours the deluded.

dancers *plural noun* stairs [From Cockney *slang 'Fred Astaires'*]

> **He wez up the dancers to the lavvy like Linford Christie after that vindaloo.**
> TRANSLATION: Needs must.

dander *verb* **1** to stroll | *noun* **2** a stroll

dee¹ *verb* to do

dee² *verb* to die

deed *adjective* dead

> **You're deed reet, that dog is as deed as a doornail.**
> TRANSLATION: There is no need to bring Towser to the vet.

deek *verb* to look at [From Romany]

> **Deek thon custy mort!**
> TRANSLATION: Look at that comely maiden!

dene *noun* a valley [From Old English *denu* valley]

> **He says he looks like James**

Dean. Ah reckon he looks like Jesmond Dene!

TRANSLATION: Even the best mirror can lie.

dickerts *plural noun* acrobatics
[From *dicker to dare*]

Wor Lizzie's deeing her dickerts again with her skort tucked into her knickors.

TRANSLATION: Young Elizabeth should be bought a leotard for Christmas.

divvent *verb* do not

dog *noun* a nickname for Newcastle Brown Ale [Possibly from the euphemistic expression 'I'm going to walk the dog', meaning 'I'm off to the pub']

Ah wez on the dog aal weekend

but the hair o the dog will dee us canny.

TRANSLATION: Some people never learn.

dolly-posh *adjective* left-handed

I wez boxing a dolly-posher and he didn't half batter me reet lug.

TRANSLATION: My opponent used his left hand and now I can only hear with my left ear.

donnered *adjective* stupid [From Old Norse *duna* to thunder; so literally meaning 'thunderstruck']

If he had a beak we'd caal him Donnered Duck.

TRANSLATION: He would not have fared well on *The Krypton Factor*.

doon *preposition, adverb, adjective* down

doon-bye *preposition* down there

dor *verb* to dare

dorna *verb* to dare not

> **Ah dorna tell wor mam ah'm in the club.**
> TRANSLATION: Byker is not Bethlehem and mother has nowt in to feed three blokes on camels.

dorsent *verb* daren't

dottle *noun* (pipe) ash [From Old English *dot* a clump.]

dozened *adjective* stupid; foolish [Related to Danish *dose* to make dull]

droonded *past participle* drowned

drucken *adjective* drunk [From Old Norse *drukken*]

ducket *noun* a place to house pigeons; pigeon loft [From *dovecote*]

> **My dad loves them pigeons so much, he lives doon the ducket.**
> TRANSLATION: Father prefers feathered company to human.

duds *plural noun* clothing [From Middle English *dudde* garment; possibly also *dud* ineffectual, defective]

> **Wor Tadger gets new duds every Easter but thy are scruffy within days.**
> TRANSLATION: Boys will be boys.

dunch *or* **dunsh** *verb* to bump; push over; shoulder charge [From Old English *dencgan* to strike]

> **I like the Waltzer at the shows but me favourite is the dunching cars.**

◄ *"... me favourite is the dunching cars."*

TRANSLATION: I am of a violent disposition even at the fairground.

dyke *noun* a ditch [From Old English *dic* ditch]

GEORDIE AT HYEM

If an Englishman's home is his castle, the Geordie's physical and emotional base is 'a willow cabin by your gate' as Shakespeare had it. After a hard day's graft, or an argument with the DSS people over his dole, or a studious perusal of totally unsuitable opportunities at the Job Centre, our hero will retire to 'tek his pipe' (rest and relax) in the warmth of his hoose.

In it will be all he needs for happiness: his 'scratcher' (bed), 'yag' (fire), 'bairns' (kids) and – most vital of all – Bella, the archetypal long-suffering Geordie wife. She it is who will have ironed the *Evening Chronicle* and left it open at the racing page, put a cushion on the 'cracket' (stool) for his aching feet and will not mind if the poor lad trots up the 'dancers' (stairs) for a much-needed kip.

If the kids are 'working themselves' (being a nuisance) she might give them a playful clout around the 'lugs' (ears) or send them to the shops to do 'messages' (shopping orders). In the old days she would have organized 'tick' (credit) at the corner shop or the Coop and purchased clothes or furniture on the 'glad and sorry' (the never-never). The lady of the house was often taken for granted. Reference this sign from the 1940s in a pub in Bedlington:

HOW TO LIVE ON 30 BOB A WEEK

Weekday beer	15 shillings
Rent	Pay next week
Three o'clock cert	3 shillings
Dog's food	5 shillings
Family food	5 shillings
Weekend beer	2 shillings
Wife's beer	2 shillings
TOTAL	32 shillings*

* This would mean going into debt, so cut out the wife's beer.

All joking aside, the Geordie matriarch is still the lynchpin of our society. She it was who sweet-talked the insurance man (known as the German, Carl Back – 'Call back!') and got a good deal from the rag-and-bone man by way of money for old tatty clothes. She has also always been the focus of the legendary Geordie hospitality to strangers. My own mother Martha was an ace at this. No matter how many of my pals landed at whatever time of day or night they were plied with food and drink. There was always beer or spirits and an endless supply of broth, sausage rolls, pease pudding (yellow oleaginous snot-coloured manna) followed by 'woolly-coat' (fruit cake) and cream cakes.

Mind you, if the stranger abused the hospitality – by puking in the outside 'lavvy' (toilet) or standing on the whippet's tail – he would catch the sharp edge of mum's tongue. **'Behave yourself or I'll put a spark up yer arse.'** Translation: 'You have overstayed your welcome and should exit stage right sharpish.'

The Geordie mother would be first up in a morning and, if she was a miner's wife, would have the man of the house's clothes, boots and 'bait' (food) ready. If her man 'scunged' (dallied) due to excess of ale, feeling 'shabby' (poorly) or simple laxity, she would holler, 'It would be more to yer mense if yee stopped maakin up there and ettled yerself for work.'

With muck everywhere and only the scrubbing brush, set-pot, mangle and lashings of Dettol, Brasso and elbow grease to assist, no wonder one frequent cry was **'Divvent drop yer dottle on the proggy mat.'** Translation: 'Please do not knock your pipe out on the home-made carpet.'

eftor *preposition, adverb, conjugation*
after

elvis *adverb* always [From a northern
pronunciation of *always*, after which the
popularity of rock 'n' roll singer Elvis Presley
probably encouraged the *w* to develop into
v]. *Compare* **divvent, intiv**

"Ah elvis sleep in me lang linings." ▶

> **Ah elvis sleep in me lang linings.**
> TRANSLATION: I always keep my
> long johns on in bed.

ettle *verb* to resolve (oneself) to do
something [From Old Norse *ætla* to
think, intend]

> **Wor Sid is tone deef but he's
> ettled on being a pop singer.**
> TRANSLATION: He'll end up in the
> outtakes for *Pop Idol.*

fadge *noun* a risen loaf [From Scots, perhaps related to Old French *fais* bundle]

> **He's got a fyace like a half-baked fadge.**
> TRANSLATION: He is no oil painting.

fell *noun* a hill, mountain, or other

high land [Old English *fel*, related to Old Norse *fiall* mountain]

> **Life is nowt but fells and denes and naebody knaas what it really means.**
> TRANSLATION: Take the rough with the smooth and still die puzzled.

femmer *adjective* frail; fragile [From Old Norse *fimr* nimble.]

fettle *noun* **1** condition; state | *verb* **2** to prepare, mend, or put the finishing touches to (something) [From Old English *fetel* belt]

> **If this cuppa tea is not just reet it will put me in a reet bad fettle.**
> TRANSLATION: Poor male chauvinist diddums.

flooer *noun* a flower

foisty *adjective* musty; damp

> **I reckon granddad has deed rats in that cree it's that foisty.**
> TRANSLATION: Grandfather's shed certainly needs a clear out.

forkytail *noun* an earwig [Presumably referring to the pincer-like appendages at the base of the abdomen]

fornenst *preposition* situated against, or facing towards

fower *determiner* four

fratch *verb* to argue or quarrel

fratchy *or* **fratchety** *adjective* given to quarrelling; irritable; crotchety

> **When wor mam gets fratchety**

on washing day, keep your heed weel doon.
TRANSLATION: The hand that rocks the cradle is the hand that clouts the lug.

frozzin *adjective* frozen

fyeul *noun* a fool

gadgie *noun* a man [From Romany, *gaijo*, *gorgio* non-Romany male]

gallowa *noun* a pony [From Galloway, an area of Scotland noted for producing them]

galluses *plural noun* braces [Probably

related to *gallows* in the sense of 'something holding something up from above'.]

> **Them galluses is that tight, his troosers is at haff mast.**
>
> TRANSLATION: Time to scrap the braces and rely on a belt.

gan *verb* to go [From Old English *gangan* to go.]

> **Gannin alang the Scotswood Road tae see the Blaydon Races.**
>
> TRANSLATION: Geordie anthem.

garth *noun* a yard or garden [From Old Norse *garthr*]

> **My mother calls the garth oot the back wor meadow.**
>
> TRANSLATION: Mama is prone to exaggeration on matters material.

geet *or* **git** *adjective* great

gert, girt *or* **gurt** *adjective* great

get rang *or* **get wrang** *verb* to be told off

> **Ah got me homework rang and ah got rang off the teachor.**
> TRANSLATION: What good are GCSEs anyway?

giveower! *exclamation* stop doing that!

> **Giveower or ah'll come ower and clock yer.**
> TRANSLATION: Your behaviour will soon end in tears.

glaky *or* **glaiky** *adjective* dimwitted

gliff *noun* a fright [From Dutch *glippen*]

Yor ugly mug is enough to gliff Darth Vader.

TRANSLATION: I suggest you do not consider becoming a film star.

gowk *noun* **1** an apple core **2** a fool
[Old English *geolc* yolk. Sense 2 may also come from Old Norse *gaukr* the cuckoo]

Only a fyeul waad swally a gowk and make hissel bowk.

TRANSLATION: An apple core is not the best aid to digestion.

gowpen *noun* a handful [Old Norse *gaupn*]

Wi may nivvor have gowld in gowpens but we'll have free habbin for company.

TRANSLATION: We may never have handfuls of gold but we'll have an open house for visitors.

graffle *verb* to search for

> **Hev a graffle in dad's pockets and see if there's any shrapnel.**
> TRANSLATION: Father will not mind if we use up his loose change.

gripe *or* **grape** *noun* a garden fork [probably from Old Norse *græip* the space between the thumb and fingers.]

grozer *noun* a gooseberry [likely from French *groseille*, but compare Gaelic *groseid*]

> **He's got such a sour puss, you'd swear he had a mouthful of grozers.**
> TRANSLATION: Guess who came last in the Cheerful Chappie contest?

guffie *noun* a pig [Possibly originally an imitation of a pig's grunt]

guizer *noun* a person dressed up to celebrate Guy Fawkes Day [From Old French *guise* appearance]

gully *noun* a large domestic knife [Perhaps an alternate spelling of French *goulet* throat, possibly indicating a butcher's knife for cutting the throat of an animal]

gyp *noun* pain; bother

Me corns is givvin us some gyp the day.

TRANSLATION: Foot faults.

AH'M SCRANNY, MAMMY

There were often hard times in Geordieland. Many of the bosses in the pits and shipyards were grasping and greedy. In the mines in the 1920s savage wage cuts were imposed. The only possible course for working blokes was collective withdrawal of labour. But in times of hardship – **'When we were wiping the sweat off our brows wi the slack off our bellies'** (No translation needed) – our stout women folk came through. **'Times wez so hard I remember me granny riving (tearing) the whalebones oot of her stays (corsets) to mek soup.'** I must admit that I have never tasted corset soup, but you'll get the gist…

Going down the pit was, for men of my father's generation – born c.1910 – only part of a self-sufficient peasant lifestyle. His family had a smallholding where they kept chickens and a few pigs. In 1943, at age three, I attended an amateur pig killing straight out of *The Wild Bunch*. My cousins lassoed the victim – a fat grunting pink porker slathered in fresh mud – and one of them whacked the pig between the eyes with a sharpened chisel. With blood spurting all over the crowd of dozens of wide-eyed folk, the bleeding shrieking animal dragged four hefty lads around the allotment for ten minutes before dying. 'Some guffie that,' said my granny. 'It wiz not ready to be turned into scran for pitmen.' Note the use of the word 'guffie'. 'Pig' was never used verbally by my mother or granny; it brought bad luck. Spelling out 'P-I-G' was fine but saying the word was as bad as letting a wild bird in your house or getting a Christmas card with green on it. Any of these were thought to bring very bad luck.

After the pig was killed, the women of the Waddell clan had a great time carving up the carcase and turning 'everything but the squeak' into sausages, bacon and pork shanks. We kids were given the pig's bladder, blown up and used as a football.

Another great ritual time was the annual September Leek Show. My dad would sit out all night guarding his monster leeks against potential slashers. Then he would bathe their butts in milk to bring up the whiteness and cart the lot off to the club for the judging. Special giant leeks were kept for seed, but that left dozens of 'scallions' (no-hopers) to be turned into leek soup, leek dumplings, and fried for sandwiches. My brother Derrick and I once ate so many of the latter, soaked in leek gravy, that we were both sick. 'Your eyes are bigger than your kites (bellies) yee two,' said dad.

Strangely, in 48 years down the pit, my dad never took with him any 'bait' (food) other than a tin flask of cold water and jam sandwiches. He claimed that meat or cheese made you 'bowk' (belch) and get stomach cramps – the last thing you need 'yakking' (using a pick) coal for eight tough hours in a two-foot 'cavil' (job area).

Geordie staple foods are very simple and often made up of leftovers. 'Pan hagglety', or 'pan hack', is fry-up. 'Chopp-uppy' is boiled eggs mixed with bread (from 'choppy' – cut-up hay for pit ponies). 'Stotty cakes' are the local sandwiches , and a favourite filling is ham and pease pudding. 'Boily' is called 'pobs' in Yorkshire and is warm milk and bread lumps, usually fed to invalids or poorly kiddies.

hack¹ *noun* a tool, such as a pick-axe, for cutting or chopping

hack² *verb* to drag (something)

hacky *adjective* dirty; muddy
[Perhaps referring to *hack* used as an instrument to rake dung, or as a miner's tool.]

**That bairn is that hacky ah'd
swear he's been rowling in
cacky.**
TRANSLATION: I think the child has
recently visited a cow byre.

had *or* **haad** *verb* to hold

**Haad yer rotten tongue or ah'll
borst yer gob!**
TRANSLATION: Silence is advisable
unless you'd like a visit to intensive
care.

hadaway! *exclamation* go away!;
get lost! [Apparently a pronunciation of
'hold away'.]

Hadaway and pelt shite!
TRANSLATION: Leave swiftly and
indulge in some useless occupation,
you are testing my patience.

hammers *plural noun* **get your hammers** to be punished with smacking: *Ah get me hammers if ah'm cheeky*

heed *noun, verb* head

hing *verb* to hang

> **Any more o your lip and I'll hing one on yer.**
> TRANSLATION: Would sir care for a mouthful of broken teeth?

hinny *noun* honey: an affectionate term

hintend *noun* the buttocks

> **If aah had a hintend as big as hors, I waad not be wearing a pelmet.**
> TRANSLATION: Self awareness is the touchstone of fashion.

hissell *pronoun* himself

hoaching *or* **hoatching** *adjective*
packed with people [From the Scots
verb *hotch* or *hoatch*, originally meaning
'to move in short, jerking motions'. This
was applied to moving aside on (e.g.) a bus
to make room for others, which possibly
yielded the sense 'packed with people']

> **The last bus was hoaching so I
> had to sit on the driver's knee.**
> TRANSLATION: Standing room only.

hoafie *noun* a fib [Perhaps from *half
(truth)*]

> **Yee tell more hoafies than a
> cheap watch.**
> TRANSLATION: Your nose is getting
> longer by the minute.

hoose *noun* a house

hoppings *plural noun* a fair, especially one that includes communal or folk dancing [From *hop*, referring to the lively dance steps]

> **Wor kid loves the hoppings so he can jive on the side of the Waltzer.**
> TRANSLATION: Stand by for Poser City, or what?

howay! *exclamation* come on! [Perhaps a contraction of *hadaway*]

> **Howay the lads!**
> TRANSLATION: Come on Newcastle United FC!

howk *verb* to dig up; pick out [From Old English *holc* hole, cavity]

If yee howk yer nose any harder yer brains will faal oot.

TRANSLATION: Stop that or we'll make you wear boxing gloves.

hoy 1 *verb* to throw 2 | *noun* **the hoy** 'pitch-n-toss' (the game) 3 | *phrase* **on the hoy** on a drinking spree; 'on the piss' [Perhaps from Dutch *gooien*]

hyem *noun, adverb* home: *Ah'm gan hyem.*

GEORDIE ON THE BEOR

I reckon, from research and personal experience, that we Geordies have a couple of dozen words for being 'drunk' and other words describing the effects of alcohol. What snow is to Eskimos, booze is to our lot: the ever-present factor in our dodgy environment.

My favourite one is 'peeve', a Romany word, much used in the Toon and the ex-mining districts over towards the North Sea.

Example: '**Ah wez on the peeve aal weekend an noo ah'm needing some fizzy belly pooders.**'

Translation: 'I went on the ale big-time

and now I am searching for the Andrews Liver Salts.'

Other words are 'bladdered' (completely wasted), 'mortalius' (ditto), 'palatik' (ditto again) derived from paralytic, 'possed' (suffering loss of motor control) and 'blaked' (experiencing wild eye-rolling).

There is a love/hate relationship between a Geordie and the beer. Newcastle Brown Ale, alias 'Newcy Broon' or 'Hooligan's Broth', is to us what wine was to Bacchus and his devotees – a mystic, powerful libation. When life was tough for the Greeks and Romans, booze was needed to inspire or relax. Indeed it is thought that Alexander the Great died in his early 30s thanks to over-indulgence in the *vins du pays* of his conquered territories. The heavy industry tradition of Geordieland meant that miners, shipbuilders and sea-farers often drank to forget the horrors and hardships of their daily lot.

The Broon should be taken ritually in carefully poured half-pint glasses. Wait till a creamy head develops, savour the fra-grance of ripe hops strained through old football socks, with just a hint of Spanish liquorice. Don't swill it – the Geordie nectar goes down smoothly but it is a heady brew indeed. Many's the novice who's stood up to leave after a night on the Toon only to find his legs have left already. It is not for nothing that the Broon is spoken of in hushed tones in places like Corbridge, Hexham, and Chester-le-Street.

Example: **'It was Broons aal roond till we went hyem stotting off the Ropeworks waal.'**

Translation: 'We over-indulged in the Geordie nectar and we went home like a pinball flying round a machine.'

This kind of experience produced the famous Geordie proverb:

'I had a smashing weekend on the bool; I was bowky aal day Sunday.'

Translation: 'I did the public house rounds excessively and, as Newton said, what goes down must come up.'

When I was 15 I was at a party and I drank a lot of beer and Cherry Brandy in the company of my granny, Mary-Jane, and she encouraged me thus, 'Get it doon, laddie, it'll do you good.' Then when I threw up into my dad's leek trench she patted my back saying, 'Get it *UP*, laddie, it'll do you good.' Behind her behaviour and philosophy was the theory that males needed to drink deep.

'Gadgies need a bit of recreation,' she would say.

Translation: 'Boys will be boys.'

The booziest time of the Geordie year is undoubtedly New Year, when the locals get plastered for several days in the manner of the Jocks at Hogmanay. Many revellers have so much to drink that they 'cowp their boily' ('blow their broth'). As a brief example, take this series of events that I was involved in at New Year 1974 in my home village of Lynemouth. I was sitting in my mum's house on January 3rd having been on the batter (merry-making) since December 20th. I was thinking of going back to work as a research assistant at Durham University that day. I was hung-over and completely skint. Then in walked one of my best pals, Cliff Howe, a former paratrooper, waving a postal order for seven quid.

'**We've got a set-in noo, let's mizzle ower to market day at Morpeth.**'

Translation: 'We are now in funds so we can re-commence our revels.' We mizzled good and proper…

We drank in the famous Joiners Arms at Morpeth and then had a Chinese meal. A friend gave us a lift the 30 miles to Durham where we drank more pints with rum chasers. We were so drunk that we had *ANOTHER* Chinese scran. By now it was 9.30 but Cliff was determined that we should keep drinking till closing time. '**Will'nt it be kiff when he rings that bell and we can stop snecking the bloody stuff.**' (Translation: 'Enough is as good as a feast – unless you are a Geordie.'

That is the aphorism that best sums up Geordie's paradoxical relationship with the 'bliddy beor'. That reminds me, there is another meaning of the much-used word 'bonny'. It usually means charming or canny, but has a tone of heavy sarcasm when used thus:

'Mind yee were bonny last neet!'

Translation: 'Go back to bed, you look like shite!'

intiv *preposition* into

> **Reach intiv yer pocket and get the
> beers in, 'cos yee've been hingin'
> back aal neet.**
> TRANSLATION: Scrooge is alive and
> living in the Bigg Market.

jan *verb* to look at [Romany]

jaup *verb* to joggle up or shake, especially liquid

jollup *noun* a purgative medicine; perhaps also a placebo [From *jalap*, from French, from Spanish *purga de Jalapa*,

ultimately from Aztec *Xalapan*, the source
of the medicine's active ingredient]

> **Caals hissel a doctor but all he
> gies ye for aches and pains is a
> bottle of pink jollup.**
> TRANSLATION: Physician heal
> thyself – 'cos yer deeing sod aal for
> me!

jugal *noun* a dog [Romany]

keek *verb* to peek

kep *verb, noun* catch [From Old
English *cepan*]

> **Stand close to the bat cos ah'm
> ganna bool for keps.**
> TRANSLATION: I think I am Shane
> Warne so stand by for fine edges.

ket *noun* **1** sweets **2** any food deemed to be unhealthy **3** raw or spoiled flesh or meat; offal; carrion [From Old Norse *kjot* meat or flesh (sense 3). Later applied to sweetmeats, yielding senses 1 and 2]

> **If them bairns fill up with ket they'll not eat their dinner.**
> TRANSLATION: Pray balance the children's diet.

kidda *noun* a term of endearment [Presumably from *kid*]

kiff *adjective* excellent; splendid [Perhaps related to *kif* cannabis, from Arabic *kayf* pleasure]

kittle *verb* to tickle [Old Norse *kitla* to tickle, possibily onomatopoetic]

knaa *verb* to know

knack *verb* to break (something)

> **Yee've got a canny knack of knackin things.**
> TRANSLATION: You have a talent for destruction.

kyek *or* **cyek** *noun* cake

lace *verb* to thrash [Dialect usage of *lace*, from Old French *lacier*, attributed to Latin *laciāre* to ensnare with a *lacium* (noose). It is unclear whether the sense 'to thrash' comes from this sense or the comparison of delivering several blows to an opponent with 'lacing' up]

ladge *noun* amazement: *eeh, for ladge…*

lang *adjective* long

larn *verb* to teach [From Old English *leornen*]

leazes *plural noun* pasture belonging to the people of a town [From Old English *læs* or Old Norse *lāth*, property]

liggie *noun* a marble [Perhaps from *liggies* testicles, though we would expect the euphemism to be the other way round. 'Liggies' are also wooden quoits used as pieces in certain games]

lolly *noun* a tongue [Perhaps related to *lollipop*, which is often licked rather than bitten]

**Divvent yee flash yer lolly at me,
or I'll bray yer.**

TRANSLATION: An eye for an eye
and a fist for a tongue.

lonnen *or* **lonnin** *noun* a wooded
lane [From the Northern pronunciation of
loaning, equivalent of *loan* lane]

lop *noun* a flea [probably from the
(unattested) Old Norse *hloppa*, from *hlaupa*
to leap]

lowey, lowie *or* **lower** *noun*
money [From Romany *luvvo* or *lovo*]

lowp *verb* **1** to jump | *noun* **2** a
jump [From Old Norse *hlaupa* to leap]

**He's turned the Slow Foxtrot into
the Rabbit Lowp.**

TRANSLATION: He will never appear
on Strictly Come Dancing.

lug *noun* an ear [Probably from Old
Norse: the word *lugg* likely meant a handle,
or something to grab hold of and pull,
echoed in the modern English *to lug*, and
modern Swedish *lugga* to pull someone's
hair]

GEET GEORDIE JUICERS

Much of my perception of the Geordie character has been based on observations in licensed premises since roughly 1956. Tossers, lossers, bossers and dossers I have seen aplenty in pubs reaching from Morpeth to the fair city of Durham.

My boozy Odyssey began when I was 15 and featured what I consider the best boozer in all of Geordieland. It stands over the way from the historic castle keep at Morpeth and is called The Joiners Arms. The bar area is a veritable cathedral to toping: on the walls are photos of great professional runners, all greased up and wearing leather jock straps. Stuffed hawks and owls peer down on generations of Morpeth wide boys 'bumming the tale' (telling tall stories) and here I learned to drink cloudy scrumpy at seven pence a pint with the Morpeth Grammar School Old Boys rugby team.

A few years later I became a fully-affiliated member of Lynemouth Social Club. Round about 1960 this was the showbiz Mecca of East Northumberland. By six o'clock on Sunday nights a queue of over 100 folk would be gathering to watch turns in the Big End. Around nine they would break out beetroot sandwiches as some local group murdered 'Twist and Shout'. Then I would execute a nifty Valeta on the dance floor with my mum Martha. Who needs Vienna?

I had a lot of coal-mining pals in Ashington and we'd meet on Fridays at the Premier (pronounced Pry-meer) down the Long Wall near the Arcade. In the big lounge a bunch of jolly boys from Pont Street used to take us to the cleaners at darts and dominoes and then we'd shoot upstairs to try and score before the Last Waltz. There was a great MC who dressed like a lounge lizard and sang 'Tangerine' and was the fastest bingo-caller in Geordieland.

I lived in Durham City for a couple of years from 1962 and was a regular at The Dun Cow in the shadow of the prison. Tommy Wilson, the landlord, sold the best pint of beer I've ever tasted – frothy Flowers bitter. Tom was on terms of matey insult with his eclectic clientele and was my shove-ha'penny partner. The standard of play was world-class, especially when Billy Mitchell played 'Dealer Boots' Melvin. The pub also featured snuff-taking competitions, and I remember one bloke sniffing two feet of Kendal Mint off the mantelpiece. He then sneezed himself daft for half an hour.

Turning to the Toon itself, the best traddy bar down the Quayside area to me is the Crown Posada, which has a great collection of sailors' hats. There are also a few football pubs worth dropping in on: the Trent Arms and the Strawberry near St James's Park. But for real footy chat I recommend the Bacchus doon a ginnel near the Theatre Royal. Air your views by all means but do not mention the Mackems after your third pint.

maak *noun* **1** a louse; bedbug | *verb*
2 to laze in bed: *yee wor lyin
maakin in bed and you slept the
caller* [Probably from Old Norse *maðkr*
maggot]

Mackem *noun* a person from
Sunderland or Wearside [Most likely

referring to the shipyards of Sunderland:
Sunderlanders 'mak 'em' (the ships) and
Geordies 'tak 'em' to sea.]

> **If the Toon keep playing like
> drains, ah'm ganna start
> supporting the Mackems.**
> TRANSLATION: Patience is a virtue,
> not a life sentence.

Mackemland *noun* Wearside

mafted *or* **mafting** *adjective*
oppressively hot; stifling

> **He hoyed so much coal on
> the fire we were aal mafted in
> minutes.**
> TRANSLATION: This is wor cosy
> little hyem, not a blacksmith's shop.

mak *or* **myek** *verb* to make

Hey there mister baker man, mak
us a cyek as fast as yer can.
TRANSLATION: A girdle scone would
go down a right treat.

man *noun* any person (not
necessarily male)

The way ye are using that broom,
man, anybody would think yee
were a woman, man.
TRANSLATION: A man's a man for
aal that.

manniskee *noun* a woman
[Romany]

marr *verb* to fight [Dialect use of
English *mar*, originally to hinder or cause
harm to]

marra *noun* a friend; pal [Perhaps
related to Old Norse *margr* friendly]

mask *verb* to brew (tea) [Perhaps a northern pronunciation of *mash*, which could be used to mean 'infuse']

mazer *noun* an eccentric or remarkable person [From dialect pronunciation of *amaze*; thus *mazer* = 'one who amazes (others)']

> **Wor Tot's a mazer, he's got hairs on his feet.**
> TRANSLATION: Thomas is a lucky person.

mebbees *adverb, sentence substitute* maybe

mell *noun* a sledgehammer [From Anglo-Norman *mail* hammer, ultimately from Latin *malleus*]

mense *noun* good manners;

propriety [From Old Norse *mennska* humanity]

> **It would be more to your mense if ye'd tek your cap off at the dinner table.**
>
> **TRANSLATION:** Father is set in his ways even when we have company.

messell *pronoun* myself

mind *verb* to remember

mint *adjective* outstanding; excellent [Probably from *mint* place where money is coined, or *mint condition*]

> **Uncle Jonty is a mint gadgie, he gis yer coppers even when he's sober.**
>
> **TRANSLATION:** My uncle does not share the prevailing view on financial matters.

mizzle¹ *noun* fine, persistent rain
[Perhaps related to Middle Dutch *misel*, a drizzling rain]

mizzle² *verb* to run away; flee
[Perhaps related to Shelta *misli* to go]

Monkeyhanger *noun* a person from Hartlepool [From the folk tale concerning the hanging of a monkey as a French spy during the Napoleonic wars]

> **We might be shy of foreigners here in the Toon, but we are not Monkeyhangers.**
> TRANSLATION: The folk of Hartlepool certainly do not welcome strangers – or circuses.

mort *noun* a woman [Perhaps from Romany but also possibly related to Middle Dutch *motte* sow.]

mozzy *noun* a midge or other stinging fly [A shortening of *mosquito*]

> **Wor Mozzy has just stuck a mozzy doon his sister's cozzy.**
> TRANSLATION: Our Morris is no paragon of correct behaviour.

nash *noun* **do a nash** to run away; flee [Romany]

> **…when the polis come alang and we did a nash.**
> TRANSLATION: He who turns and runs away…

neet *noun* night

netty *noun* a toilet [perhaps from Old English *nid* necessity]

nithered *adjective* feeling cold; chilled [From Old English *niðerian* to lower]

> **The wind is like a knife and ah'm fair nithered.**
> TRANSLATION: Oot the way of that fire.

nivvor *adverb* never

> **Nivvor in the creation of crow's droppings have I seen a sight like yee. Yee've been on the hoy too lang.**
> TRANSLATION: The Primrose Path leads only to perdition.

noo *adverb, conjugation* now

"We did a nash when the polis came."

nool *or* **knowl** *verb* to beat
(somebody) down; cow (somebody)
[Perhaps related to Scots *knool* to strike or
punch with the knuckles]

> **Thon teacher has the bairns aal
> nooled; they're too scared to raise
> their hands even if they knaa the
> answer.**
> TRANSLATION: Mailed Fist 1
> – Velvet Glove 0.

noo then *sentence substitute* hello;
how are you?

nowt *noun* nothing

nyem *noun, verb* name

nyeuk *noun* a nook

GEORDIE ON THE PULL

When I was a lad in Ashington circa 1956 I was taught the art of chatting up ladies by a bunch of wide boys at Docherty's billiard hall.

Through the week you had to look like an extra from *West Side Story*, chew gum and speak out of the corner of your gob. Then on Saturday night it was Italian suits, winkle pickers and full-on smarmy gigolo patter. The first aim was **'to score with a bord'** – Translation: 'to impress a girl'. Here are a few ways me and my marras (mates) tried to work the magic.

'For a big lassie yee divvent sweat that much.'

Translation: 'You are of Reubenesque proportions but you get ten out of ten for personal hygiene.'

Mind you, the lasses could hit you back with some belters.

'Haddaway and pelt; if patter was watter yee'd be droonded.'

Translation: 'Leave the environs of my person; you may have the gift of the gab but I would not trust you as far as I could spit cannonballs.'

Another rebuff by the locals lasses could occur if you had failed to shower recently.

'Yee luk canny gud, but yee shud hoy scent under yer oxters if yee want to score heor.'

Translation: 'You are a fit specimen of manhood but a deodorant would enhance your charms no end.'

Much of this interaction took place in dance halls and there was a kind of code in the simplest of statements.

'Do yee fancy gannin for a Chinese after the hop?'

Translation: 'I am a generous lad and willing to invest money in our relationship – and I fancy a snog in the back lane.'

In the Alnwick area a fast-witted mort (lass) might reply thus:

'Aah naa it's not scran yer after, gadgie, but you look like a shan jugal to me.'

Translation: 'Your motives are obvious, pal, and I reckon you are a dirty dog'.

At a dance at Amble one of my hawker mates once said this as a shapely girl walked past **'Deekie for ladge the case on that!'**

Translation: 'My goodness me, that girl wiggles like a sack full of baby bunnies.'

Geordies are marvellous exaggerators when engaging in sensual spiel. One Toony mate of mine at Cambridge tried this line on a blue-stocking swot at a soiree.

'You look that kiff that I could make a meal out of your pop of the hask.'

Translation: 'I know a form of tonsil hockey that would make you swoon.' Cue frozen lip and swan away.

Moving to the present, Newcastle's popularity as a party city for Hens, Stags, and students means that the chat is even more sophisticated now – but still couched in the racy vernacular. I am told that the belly-toppers (lasses wearing nowt from chest to belly-button) are very aggressive with it if they spot a fit bloke.

Example: **'Ah've got a fella back yem**

who's a peely-wally worky-ticket but your geet canny and I'm not superstitious.'

Translation: 'My regular boyfriend is a major disappointment so you could be in luck tonight.'

If by chance you are on a Stag outing to the Quayside, here are couple of chat-up lines that might endear you to the local lasses.

'Ah've got a load of tabs and a poke full of lowey and we can gan on the hoy.'

Translation: 'I have fags and plenty of readies, so we can cast care aside and have a jolly time.'

'You are as custy as a stotty and as tasty as a fresh willick.'

Translation: 'You make my mouth water as much as fresh baked bread and salted whelks'.

The best places to try this patter are the ritzy bars on the river and the traddy pubs in the Bigg Market. Bon chance, as they say in Byker.

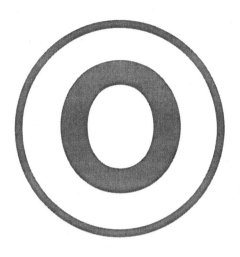

ony *adjective* any

> **Has ony onyer ony lowey onyer?**
> TRANSLATION: I am in need of a
> financial sub.

oor *noun* hour

oot *adverb* out

ower *preposition, adverb* over

owld *adjective* old

oxter *noun* the armpit [From Old
English oxtā]

paaky *or* **pawky** *adjective* choosy
[From *pawk* a trick or ruse. Its current
usage has possibly been influenced by *picky*]

> **Can ah tek yer hyem from the dance, pet – ah'm not paaky.**
> TRANSLATION: I do not have a GSCE in chatting-up.

pagger *verb* to tire or exhaust (someone or something); to beat [From Romany]

> **Sum buggaz paggered the hole in the waal, so ah'm sponned for spondies.**
> TRANSLATION: I hope the public house extends credit because I am now short of the readies.

palatick *adjective* drunk [Shortening of *paralytic*]

panhaggerty *or* **panacalty** *noun* a common dish made of leftover meat and potatoes

> **Wor mother should not booze while cooking; she's turned steak aux poivre into panhaggerty.**

pany *noun* water

> **This tea is so weak it's good pany wasted.**
> TRANSLATION: Don't be so paaky with the teabags.

patter *noun* speech, talk, chat etc

pay *verb* to beat (someone) in a fight

peely-wally *adjective* (of a person) pallid

> **Yee are as peely-wally as unfried tripe.**
> TRANSLATION: Have you seen a ghost or just got the gas bill for the winter quarter?

peevy *adjective* drunk [From Romany *peava* a drink]

pet *noun* a casual term of endearment [Probably dialect usage of *pet*. A shortening of *petal* has also been suggested]

petal *or* **petal-flower** *noun* a casual term of endearment

pezzle *verb* to bash [From *pestle*]

> **Yee couldn't pezzle yer way oot of a plastic carrier bag.**
> TRANSLATION: You are as weak as chip-shop vinegar.

pikelet *noun* a kind of crumpet [From Welsh *bara pyglyd* dark bread, referring to the colour of crumpets]

Pitmatic *noun* a dialect spoken in the coal-mining areas of the North East [From *pit* + -*matic* (formed by analogy with *mathematic*]

pittle *verb* **1** to urinate | *noun* **2** urine [Related to *piddle*]

> **Wees cowped the pittle pail?**
> TRANSLATION: Who has tipped over the night-time urinary facility.

ploat *verb* to pluck [Related to Dutch *ploten* to pluck]

> **It teks hor langer to ploat her eyebrows than it does to dee the Christmas torkey.**
> TRANSLATION: Wor lass is very particular about her appearance.

plodge *verb* to wade; trudge (as through mud, etc) [An alternate form of *plod*]

plooky *adjective* (of the face) spotty; covered with acne [From Middle

English *plouke* or Middle Scots *pluik*,
pimple.]

> **Me face is as plooky as a pack o
> dominoes.**
> TRANSLATION: I have volcanic acne.

poke *noun* a wallet; stash [From
Anglo-Norman or Old French *poque*, bag.]

pollis *noun* the police; a police
officer

pop of the hask *noun* the uvula
[Possibly related to *harsh* or *husky*, the
latter especially being applicable to a
cough]

> **He's taalkin as though his pop of
> the hask was lathered with tar.**
> TRANSLATION: Break out the Friar's
> Balsam and boil the kettle.

poss *verb* **1** to pound (washing)
2 to physically beat (someone)
[Possibly related to *push* or French *pousser*]

proggy mat *noun* a homemade
carpet

puggle *adjective* daft [Compare the
Scots word *puggled* meaning 'very drunk',
purportedly from Hindustani *pagal* 'mad']

radge *or* **radgie** *adjective*
1 furious; raging **2** stupid [From Romany *raj* stupid, crazy; or perhaps an alteration of *rage*]

> **Wor baker might be fadge-faced, but he's not radge.**
> TRANSLATION: Our local baker is prone to sharp practices.

rax *verb* to stretch [From Old English *raxan*]

reed *adjective, noun* red

reet *adjective, adverb, noun* right

> **Tornin reet might be reet, but mebbees torning left might be reet.**
>
> TRANSLATION: I suggest you buy a map, my parsimonious Southern friend.

rive *verb* to rip or tear; take by force

> **There was nee need to rive the Chronicle off us, noo yee've torn it.**
>
> TRANSLATION: What are we going to wrap the chips in now?

rowl *verb, noun* roll

"Wor baker's not radge."

GEORDIE SPORTS (INCLUDING FIGHTING)

Most sociologists agree that modern sports like football, cricket, rugby and even darts are ritualized and less harmful descendants of warfare. In the case of football there is strong evidence that after trans-border clashes between the English Robsons and the Scottish Humes around 1650, football matches were played using the heads of dead enemies as the ball. There is plenty of blood, snot and jeers when Sunderland take on the Toon at football today, but things rarely get as bad as deliberate decapitation…

Before looking in detail at some of wor favourite sports, I will remind you that there are more Geordie words for fighting and hitting than there are for drink!

Here are some of the most evocative: 'bray' – thrash; 'pezzle' – pound; 'dunch' – shoulder charge; 'batter' – shower blows; 'yark' – smack heavily; 'pagger' – make tired through hitting; 'marr' – fight as a group, as in 'marras'; 'hammers', as in 'I'll give yee yer hammers'. This latter is what some power-mad school teachers used to get away with in the bad old days. I also remember some hectic Saturday inter-family fights in our back lane after drunken Saturday nights. You knew it was getting serious when somebody yelled

'Fetch yer aad yins out.'

Translation: 'Bring out reinforcements

in the form of grannies and granddads.'

Given the plethora of violent words in our domestic and working lives, no wonder that football crowds in Geordieland use the language of the battlefield in these so-called civilized times. Here are some examples from visits to St James' Park and other grounds over the years.

I first went to see the Toon about 1947 as a skinny seven-year-old with my Uncle Sam, who wore proudly the uniform and blood red hackle (feather badge) of the Royal Northumberland Fusiliers. We were a bit late taking our places high on the Leazes End banking. Even on tiptoes I could not see a thing. Then a rough voice shouted **'Lift the laddie up-a-height and we'll rowl him doon the front.'** Translation: 'That boy deserves a ringside seat'.

Next thing I knew I was rolled like a new stairs carpet over the heads of the crowd and deposited on the cinder track, smelling Broon fumes from behind me and wintergreen from the players' legs.

At Roker Park in the 1950s we always went with the motto 'We aren't half ganna pagger the Mackems today. The Toon will crucify them.' And indeed with chunky Jimmy Scoular playing for us and craggy Billy Elliot for them in midfield, blood was often spilt. At one gruesome derby the ball flew high into the stand and was lost. At which one Toon supporter yelled:

'Forget the bliddy ball – get on with the gyem.'

Translation: 'We have not come to see art, we've come to see carnage.'

Then again, going to the match was kind

of duty, a traumatic pilgrimage. I had heard the motto about the 'savage amusement' inherent in pinning your faith to Newcastle United. It went like this: 'We could pezzle Brazil on a Monday and get paggered by Blyth Spartans on a Wednesday.' And on a stormy day in late 1967 I was party to all the tragicomic theatre that being a Toon supporter involves. Our opponents were Manchester United and their forward line was Best, Law, Charlton, Kidd, Aston – a line-up that could batter Brazil 6-0. Fingers were crossed and black-and-white scarves tautened to throttling point.

But, by oceans of luck and some kamikaze defending, we were 2-0 up with ten minutes to go. Most teams could sew things up from here, but not our lads. Thousands of grown men were turning their faces to the sky screaming, 'Blaa the bliddy whistle.' But the Man Above did not hear. Charlton hit the bar, Kidd hit the post. They got two goals, but it could have been six, no bother. It was a 2-2 draw. We had not been humiliated; we had given as good as we got.

We danced down the Gallowgate to the boozers as if we had won the FA Cup.

Another sport that my father's generation used to take part in was 'foot running', so labelled to distinguish it from dog – i.e. whippet – racing. Good runners were kept off work and sex for weeks, trained exactly like prize whippets or greyhounds, fed steak and milk, then unleashed against all-comers. The runners were handicapped and hundreds of pounds of family money went on the betting. Sadly for the Waddell clan, our champion who ran under the assumed name of 'Raymond of Cresswell' (definitely a touch of the Crufts there) was great in training but did not have the temperament to handle the pressure of race day. So the cry would go up:

'Raymond took the watter in agyen, flew like a linty wi a broken wing.'

Translation: 'Raymond did not prevail. He flew like a crippled linnet.'

To end this section on a sad note, around 1964 a bloke in Ashington had a young whippet that cost him a fortune to buy, feed, and train but it could never win a race. So one day he got fed up and sold the dog to a local Chinese restaurant who served up the whippet as best chicken chow mein. The story got out and the restaurant was done for it. Pity there were no Chinese restaurants about in the late 1930s when wimpy Raymond of Cresswell was on the go!

sackless *adjective* useless [From Old Norse *saklaus*]

scran *noun* **1** food | *verb* **2** to eat

scranchings *noun* hard fish batter [Of debatable origin but possibly cognate with Flemish *schranzen*]

scumfish *verb* to smother or stifle; choke [Scots]

> **Open the bliddy windows or we'll aal scumfish.**
> TRANSLATION: We do *NOT* need more coal on that fire.

scunge *noun* to snooze

> **If yee lie scunging in that scratcher any langer ye'll turn into a bed bug.**
> TRANSLATION: Get up and face the day.

scunner *verb* to scowl

> **If yee scunner any harder yer neb will touch yer chin.**
> TRANSLATION: Report for duty at the Punch and Judy Show.

set-in *noun* an amount of money just sufficient to get one started on a drinking spree that one hopes will be sustained by the generosity of other drinkers [From *set* in the sense of 'start (someone) on their way']

> **Afore wi set oot, wi bettor get a set in, or they'll caal us cadgers.**
> TRANSLATION: The wheels of charity may need a little oiling.

shan *adjective* bad; below par [Perhaps from Romany]

> **Wearing a spotty top with a stripey skirt is deed shan.**
> TRANSLATION: She must have put on that ensemble in the dark.

shuggy-boat *noun* a type of fairground swing [Related to Scots *shoogle*, shake, ultimately from *shog*]

singin' hinny *noun phrase* a kind of currant bun that emits a singing noise when cooked on a griddle

skelp *verb* to thrash or beat [Probably related to Icelandic *sklefa*]

skemmy *noun* a common pigeon, especially one that is weak or lacking in vigour

> **He's aboot as much use as a skemmy wearing diving byeuts.**
> TRANSLATION: This dog won't hunt.

Smoggie *noun* a person from Teesside

> **Ah divvent knaa how the Smoggies drink that Strongarm beer – it makes me bowk.**
> TRANSLATION: Whether it's ale or lasses, stick to what yer used to.

sneck *noun* **1** a door or gate latch **2** the nose [Perhaps from Middle English *snek* latch]

> **He banged his sneck on the backyard sneck and now he's snooking blood.**
> TRANSLATION: His accident has badly affected his olfactory region.

snook *verb* **1** to inhale through the nose with short, rapid breaths; sniff | *noun* **2** the nose [Perhaps from Old Norse]

spelk *noun* a splinter [From Old English *spelc*]

spon *verb* **1** to cheat **2** to hinder

> **Wor whippet is limping, so that's us sponned at the sweep.**

TRANSLATION: Our sporting investment just went belly up.

spondies *plural noun* money [From 'spondulicks']

> **No spondies means its fireside and fry-ups this weekend.**
> **TRANSLATION:** We will not be joining the beau monde at the Eldon Grill.

spuggy *noun* a sparrow [Compare Scots *spug, spurg*]

squitts *adjective* quits (even)

> **Yee smacked me sneck and I bloodied yer gob, so that make us squitts.**
> **TRANSLATION:** A nose for a nose, a lip for a lip.

stays *plural noun* a corset

> **If granny keeps deein the Twist she'll borst her stays.**
> TRANSLATION: Once a raver, always a raver.

stot *verb* to rebound; to make something bounce [Probably related to Dutch *stoten*]

> **Work? I'd rather try to stot a warm stotty off a wet beach.**
> TRANSLATION: I do not see the point of gainful employment with its risk to my soundness of body.

stottie *or* **stottie-kyek** *noun* a cake of flat, unrisen bread [Perhaps from *stot* (see above), as in a resilient yeast-based cake]

stowed-out *adjective phrase* full to

bursting [Probably from *stow* to fill by
packing + *out* finished, exhausted]

> **The Big End is stowed-out, you
> couldn't squeeze an eel covered
> in Vaseline in.**
> TRANSLATION: The
> Shoowaddywaddy tribute band is
> very popular.

stumor *noun* **1** a remarkable or
uncanny person or action **2** a
foolish person or action [Possibly
from the Scandinavian root *stum* mute, thus
referring to a person whose actions strike
one dumb]

> **Wor Lizzie is a stumor, she's got
> the lads tumbling aal ower her.**
> TRANSLATION: Elizabeth never has
> to buy a drink or pay herself into the
> pictures.

taak *verb* to talk

> **Everybody's taaking at me, but ah dain't hear a word they're saying…**
> (Line from song in movie 'Monkseaton Midnight Cowboy'.)

tab *noun* a cigarette [From the cigarette brand *Ogden's Tabs*]

Keep tabs on how many tabs she hez, or she'll be coughing her guts up.
TRANSLATION: Some people lose all perspective on social occasions.

tadger *noun* **1** a child **2** a tadpole **3** a penis [Origin unknown, but some suggest it is a shortened form of *tadpole*]

tak *verb* to take

If ye tak somebody's hospitality, mek sure yee divvent tak a lend.
TRANSLATION: Don't bite the hand that feeds or pours.

tappy-lappy *adjective, adverb* headlong; willy-nilly; quickly and recklessly

So Moses whacked the watter, the Red Sea parted and aal the

"They booled tappy-lappy into the Promised Land." ▶

> **Israelites and their lasses booled tappy-lappy into the Promised Land.**
> TRANSLATION: Jerusalem or bust.

tettie *noun* **1** a potato **2** a hole in a sock through which the foot is visible [Geordie pronunciation of *tattie*, short for *potato*]

> **Yer socks hez more tetties than me granny's shepherd's pie.**
> TRANSLATION: Time to open a Co-op account for new footwear.

thon *determiner* yon [From earlier *yon*, remodelled to conform with *this* and *that*]

thorsells *pronoun* themselves

thropple *noun* the throat [Some suggest it is a combination of Old English *throte* throat + *bolla* boll (bud or rounded pod)]

tidy-betty *noun* a fender (in front of a fireplace)

tit-and-fiddle end *noun* the snug (in a public house or club). *Compare* **big end**

tiv *preposition* to. *Compare* **intiv**

Toon *noun* **the Toon** Newcastle [Northern pronunciation of *town*]

toot *noun* **1** *Also* **tooter** a spy; a voyeur | *verb* **2** to spy **3 keep toot** to act as a lookout [Purportedly from Old English *tutan* or *tūjan*, meaning to peep or peek out]

> **I was tooting on a courting couple when he copped us and giv us me hammers.**
>
> TRANSLATION: I spy with my little

black eye something beginning with 'F'… for fist!

trot *or* **trots** *noun* **1** a long rope for raising and lowering tubs in a coal pit **2** a fishing line

tussy-pegs *plural noun* teeth

twank *verb* to spank, smack (a child) as punishment

twelt *verb* to strike (a ball) with a bat

tyek *verb* to take

varnigh *adverb* almost; nearly
[Coalescence of *varry* very + *nigh* nigh or nearly]

The barber varnigh sliced me lug off!
TRANSLATION: I didn't ask for a short back and ears!

varry *adverb* very

**Ah'm varry varry sorry the club
trip has been cancelled, but the
funds have mizzled alang with
half the committee.**

TRANSLATION: Apocryphal sign in
working men's club.

waak *verb* to walk

> **WORK, him. He cannit even WAAK!**
>
> TRANSLATION: Yonder is a person to whom honest toil is anathema.

warse *adjective, adverb* worse

weel *adjective, adverb* well

Why aye! *interjection* of course, certainly

> **Why aye I'll give yer the benefit of the doot, but yer deed wrang!**
> TRANSLATION: I am an open-minded unprejudiced person.

willick *noun* a whelk; winkle [From Old English *wioloc*]

wor *determiner* our

work yersel *verb* to act up

worky-ticket *noun* a layabout [The phrase purportedly originates from Tyneside Railways, where it was used to describe a troublesome customer]

yacker *noun* a hewer of coal [Origin uncertain. Some suggest a connection to *hack*, others to *yark*, still others to the Australian Aboriginal *yakka* toil, hard work]

yag *noun* a fire [From Romany]

yark *verb* to hit (someone or something) with a heavy blow
[From Middle English *yerk* to hit]

OF CLUBS AND CULCHA

Some people might be surprised that I lump together the place where a Geordie goes to drink and the places he goes to refresh his emotional and artistic life. But there is no paradox. 'Gannin' doon the club' was never just an excuse for a beer or six. As one old miner with 'grog blossom' (broken veins) all over his chops told me haughtily:

'We had football teams, cricket teams, domino and darts teams, sartinly, but nivvor drinking teams.'

In 1964 I did a study of the 27 work-ingmen's clubs in Ashington for the

Workers' Educational Association. From the Fell 'em Doon at the top end to the Premier, part of the Long Wall – five consecutive licensed premises – at the bottom end, I found glass cases full of books next to the sports trophy cabinets in seven of them. Here mouldered the works of John Stuart Mill and Adam Smith, a tribute to the days when miners tried to better themselves.

The clubs also encouraged a fashion code that would not have been out of place in Jermyn Street or Belgravia. Take my father's Sunday morning ritual circa 1960. Wash and shave carefully with a cut-throat razor. Apply Brylcreem to thinning hair. Put on white shirt with stiff collar and tie. Hang on watch and chain. Put on black shoes, shined by mother. At the end he looked like a minister in Ramsay

MacDonald's first Labour cabinet. He did not approve of my jeans, the back pocket of which was held on by a rusty safety pin. 'You're not showing me up at the club like a 'guizer' (Halloween dresser-up) with your 'britchy arse' (backside) hanging out.' I took the point and went along dressed in a pair of his old moleskin work pants.

And what was the aim of all this? Answer: to sit in the Big End at Lynemouth Social Club supping warm Federation Special, eating complimentary cheese, pickles and black pudding… and playing bingo! After that there was a 'Go As You Please' with singers from the members and a bloke who took his teeth out and did Popeye impressions. Their reward – pink pint tickets dished out by committee men.

The Ashington group of Pitmen

Painters, led by Oliver Kilbourn, and now made famous in a play by Lee Hall, author of *Billy Elliot*, made the club, the home, and the workplace the subjects of their art. They painted whippets, 'crees' (sheds), pit props, and sweating ponies. In the 1940s their exhibition was seen and approved by millions of Chinese people. We have other top artists. Norman Cornish of Spennymoor created gnarled and twisted miners going to work like storm-blown trees and Morpeth's Malcolm Teasdale renders the rain-spattered streets of Tyneside and the shivering football terraces with a heartfelt accuracy.

All-in-all there's a canny lot to seek out and appreciate in Geordieland. – '**Tek this byuk wii yer and yer'll dee alreet.**' Translation: 'Bon voyage.'

About the author

The son of a miner, Sid Waddell was born in Alnwick, Northumberland, and attended King Edward VI grammar school where he excelled at rugby and athletics. He won a scholarship to St John's College, Cambridge, where he read modern history. An injury curtailed his outdoor sporting pursuits but gave him the opportunity to concentrate on indoor sports, organizing the first Intercollegiate Darts Championship.

After university, Sid joined Granada Television and worked on a number of documentaries. He moved to Yorkshire television in 1972, where he created the show *Indoor League*, bringing darts to television for the first time. In 1976 he joined the BBC and was a commentator on the first World Professional Darts Championship when it began two years later. For the next sixteen years, Sid was the BBC's main darts commentator, becoming a well-known and popular broadcaster and acquiring something of a cult following among sports fans. He moved to Sky Sports in the mid-1990s, continuing to commentate on darts as well as adding pool and clay pigeon shooting to his broadcasting repertoire. Over the years his unmistakeable voice and unique style of commentary – an effortless mix of deep sporting knowledge, classical references, and surreal flights of fancy – have made him a much-loved and respected television personality.

Sid has written eleven books, including a number of biographies of his favourite sportsmen. He has also created two successful children's comedy series in *Jossy's Giants* and *Sloggers*.

A true Geordie, with both 'Pitmatic' and 'Gadgie' blood in his veins, Sid has always been interested in the language and lore of the North East. Although he has previously published a book on Yorkshire dialect, this is his first book on Geordie.